The Price of Stability...?

*A study of price fluctuations in primary products
with alternative proposals for stabilisation*

SIR SYDNEY CAINE

Published by

THE INSTITUTE OF ECONOMIC AFFAIRS

1983

First published in March 1983

by

The Institute of Economic Affairs
2 Lord North Street, Westminster
London SW1P 3LB

ISSN 0073-2818
ISBN 0-255 36160-2

Printed in England by

GORON PRO-PRINT CO LTD

6 Marlborough Road, Churchill Industrial Estate, Lancing, W. Sussex

Text set in 'Monotype' Baskerville

CONTENTS

[4]

PREFACE

The *Hobart Papers* are intended to contribute a stream of authoritative, independent and lucid analyses to the understanding and application of economics to private and government activity. The characteristic theme has been the optimum use of scarce resources and the extent to which it can best be achieved in markets within an appropriate framework of law and institutions or, where markets cannot work, in other ways. Since in the real world the alternative to the market is the state, and both are imperfect, the choice between them effectively turns on a judgement of the comparative consequences of 'market failure' and 'government failure'.

Nowhere is this choice more clearly demonstrated than in the production and sale of primary products. The marked fluctuation in prices of many commodities is widely regarded as an example of 'market failure', not in the sense that prices do not work, but rather that they work too vigorously and lead to unacceptable consequences.

As a result, governments have for many years considered a variety of schemes to restrict, or even replace, the price mechanism, including marketing boards, bulk purchase, quota agreements, buffer stock and compensation schemes. But the persistent lack of success of government initiatives may be judged from the ever-growing demand, voiced in the so-called 'North-South' debate, that Western governments should do still more to help the Third World, which is usually, if mistakenly, thought to be synonymous with the primary producing countries. The two Brandt Reports, the creation of UNCTAD, and the long debate on the economic development of poor countries, all share a common ancestry. It was the World Economic Conference, held in London in 1933, which produced the first set of principles to guide governments trying to introduce regulation and control of commodities.

It seemed timely, therefore, to review and assess the attempts made during the last 50 years to bring about more stable prices, and it was clearly appropriate for the Institute to invite Sir Sydney Caine to take further the analysis of his earlier

Hobart Paper 24, *Prices for Primary Producers,* written in 1963 and revised in 1966. Sir Sydney is uniquely qualified to undertake this task, having combined a lifetime's study of economics, including a special knowledge of international commodity markets, with practical experience of colonial administration.

At the start, Sir Sydney asks for clarity about objectives from those who call for regulation. Is their purpose to smooth out fluctuations in prices, or to raise their average level? Is it to bring production and consumption into balance, or to evoke a particular pattern of income distribution?

Sir Sydney reminds us that primary products do have special characteristics, since they may be vulnerable to the weather, or require a substantial capital investment which takes many years to reach maturity. Nevertheless, primary products still respond to changes in price, however slowly, even if the combination of heavy long-term capital costs and low current costs can for a time produce a perverse reaction, by maintaining the volume of supplies even after a severe fall in prices.

Not only do few of the many official regulatory schemes introduced in the last 50 years seem to have succeeded, but Sir Sydney points out that some of the difficulties have even been aggravated by government. The restrictions by industrialised countries on their imports of primary products, for example, has contracted the market for exports from developing countries. Thus employment on West Indian sugar-cane plantations has been destroyed by the subsidisation of higher-cost sugar-beet farmers in East Anglia and elsewhere in the EEC.

Among the recommendations are proposals to widen the market by reducing the proportion reserved for protected producers, and to improve the flow of information about market trends. Sir Sydney also makes a novel proposal for a Long-Term Contract Agency, which might act as a broker in arranging contracts for longer periods than currently available through existing commodity exchanges, though without inhibiting the fundamental role of the market in allocating resources.

The Institute is not committed to this or any other of the conclusions of Sir Sydney's analysis, but it offers his *Hobart Paper* as an authoritative contribution to a discussion which is all the more urgent at a time when international trade and payments are coming under an unprecedented strain, bringing with it the threat of a return to protectionism.

February 1983   JOHN B. WOOD

THE AUTHOR

SIR SYDNEY CAINE, K.C.M.G., HON. LL.D. (University of Malaya), was born in 1902 and educated at Harrow County School and the London School of Economics (B.Sc. (Econ.) First Class Hons., 1922), of which he later became Director. Between 1923 and 1952 he was in government service, mainly in the Colonial Office, which he entered in 1926. He was secretary of the West Indian Sugar Commission, 1929; and of the UK Sugar Industry Inquiry Committee, 1934. He served as financial secretary in Hong Kong, 1937-39; financial adviser to the Secretary of State, Colonial Office, 1942; and successively assistant under-secretary and deputy under-secretary at the Colonial Office, 1944-48, followed by a period in the Treasury during which he headed the Treasury and Supply Delegation in Washington, 1949-51. He was knighted in 1947.

Sir Sydney turned to university administration in 1952, being Vice-Chancellor of the University of Malaya, 1952-56, before becoming Director of the LSE in 1957 until his retirement in September 1967. He was chairman of the governing body of the International Institute of Educational Planning, 1963-70, chairman of the Planning Board of the Independent University, 1969-73, then chairman of the Council after its establishment as the University College at Buckingham, 1973-76. From 1960 to 1967 he was a member and from 1964 deputy chairman of the Independent Television Authority.

Sir Sydney's publications include *The Foundation of the London School of Economics* (1963); *British Universities: Purpose and Prospects* (1969); and, for the IEA, of which he was a Trustee from April 1968 to December 1972, he has previously written *Prices for Primary Producers* (Hobart Paper 24, 1963, Second Edition 1966) and *Paying for TV?* (Hobart Paper 43, 1968, with a supplement: *Statement on TV Policy,* published in 1969). He also contributed to *Overseas Investment or Economic Nationalism?* (Occasional Paper 15, 1967).

[8]

ONE: Introduction

Concern about wide fluctuations in the prices of primary products has a long history. Currently it figures prominently in the debate on the so-called 'North-South' relationship between 'rich' and 'poor' countries. It has been particularly emphasised in proposals put forward by the United Nations Conference on Trade and Development (UNCTAD)[1] and, more recently, by the 'Brandt Commission'.[2] The discussion has always combined the two objectives of smoothing out the more violent fluctuations in prices and raising their average level. It is apparent, however, that the latter is what appeals most to supporters of the Brandt proposals and other protagonists, who assume that primary product producers are substantially synonymous with poor countries.

This *Hobart Paper* examines that and other underlying assumptions. It reviews past attempts to regulate world trade in individual commodities and the principles which have at different times been put forward as a basis for such regulation. It also discusses the practical problems of administering regulation schemes. Above all, it is concerned with the difficulties which arise from trying to use prices as a means for re-distri-

---

[1] UNCTAD emerged out of pressure from developing countries dissatisfied with the existing arrangements for international trade which, since World War II, have been regulated by the General Agreement on Tariffs and Trade (GATT). The first UNCTAD was held in Geneva from March to June 1964; it was attended by representatives of 150 nations, and was notable for the emergence of a 'Group of 77' developing countries (since expanded to over 100 members) formed to promote their economic interests jointly. The practical outcome of the Geneva conference was the establishment of UNCTAD as a permanent organ of the United Nations, charged with the duty (in the words of the UN General Assembly's resolution which created it) 'to promote international trade, especially with a view to accelerating economic development, particularly trade between countries at different stages of development . . .'. It has a permanent executive, the Trade and Development Board, and its own secretariat, based in Geneva.

The Geneva meeting set a wide-ranging agenda for trade reform, subsequently elaborated at four further meetings in New Delhi (1968), Santiago (1972), Nairobi (1976), and Manila (1979). The Sixth Session of UNCTAD is to take place in Belgrade in June 1983.

[2] *North-South: A Programme for Survival*, The Report of the Independent Commission on International Development Issues under the Chairmanship of Willy Brandt, Pan Books, London, 1980.

buting wealth rather than for balancing changes in demand and supply.

The advocates of regulation have tended in both past and current discussions to assume that supply, if not fixed irrespective of price, can be closely regulated, and that demand is inelastic. It is true that, for a number of primary products, both demand and supply have low price elasticities. But history shows that, except in some instances where a monopoly either exists or can be established, the normal reactions in supply and demand do occur if artificial prices are maintained for more than a limited period. Effective long-term control is not within the power of any worldwide authority likely to be established in the foreseeable future and, insofar as such control could be exercised, it would tend to be at the expense rather than for the benefit of countries most in need of new economic development.

On this basic assumption that market forces cannot be ignored, the *Paper* finally examines whether there are ways not yet adequately exploited of improving the operation and scope of free markets rather than trying to by-pass them.

TWO: The Problem Outlined

In 1968 the price in New York of sugar sold on the free world market was below 3 cents per lb; in 1974 it rose above 65 cents; in July 1978 it was under 7 cents. Coffee sold for under 20 cents per lb in 1947, over 150 cents in 1954, 35 cents in 1963, as much as 340 cents in 1977 and in July 1978 was quoted at about 150 cents. Tin was 100 cents per lb in 1960, 440 cents in 1974 and about 550 cents in 1978. Within four months in 1974 the price of copper fell from £1,400 per ton to £586.

Summarising the commodity position in its issue of 15 January 1983, *The Economist* noted that sugar stocks mounted during 1982 and sugar prices fell to four-year lows by the middle of the year; cocoa prices continued to drift until a prospective fall in production boosted prices in December; grain and soya bean prices weakened following bumper harvests in the USA and Europe; and palm and groundnut oil prices were the lowest since the mid-1970s, following a surplus of oilseeds production. The index of dollar prices of the principal primary products, taking 1975 prices as 100, rose to a peak of nearly 240 in 1980 and dropped back to under 150 in 1982.

Early attempts to reduce price fluctuations

Many more examples of wide fluctuations could be quoted for other commodities and from other periods. Inevitably such large fluctuations have led to much discussion of measures to eliminate or reduce them. Such discussions are by no means new. Ignoring earlier interventions in commodity markets by governments going back at least to Joseph's manipulation of the Egyptian corn market, we can discern a growing concern since the early years of this century. In 1903 the Brussels Agreement on sugar subsidies was a (reasonably successful) attempt to deal with a specific disturbance in the world sugar market. Shortly before the beginning of World War I there were discussions in Brazil (in the upshot ineffective) to prevent falls in the price of rubber and coffee. Soon after World War I

[11]

discussions began in Malaya, initially between producers but soon involving governments there and elsewhere, aimed at regulating rubber prices. These talks led to control measures which enjoyed a short-term success but passed through many vicissitudes before the moderately effective International Rubber Regulation Scheme came into operation in 1934. During the same period after World War I there were other discussions leading to agreements of varying scope and effectiveness for the international regulation of coffee, tea, sugar, tin, copper and other commodities.

All these discussions, although coming to involve governments, were initiated by producers' organisations. There emerged, however, a growing recognition of a more widespread, if not universal, concern with the problems of international commodity trade. This concern was officially formulated in a report adopted by the World Monetary and Economic Conference held in London in 1933, organised by the League of Nations and attended by representatives of the majority of member states plus the USA.[1] The principle of commodity agreements was commended by the Conference and contracts made there led to continuing discussions of individual commodity problems and, for sugar, to a wide-ranging agreement concluded in 1937 which, however, the outbreak of World War II prevented from becoming fully operative.

Incomplete success

During the 1930s and since the end of World War II, government agreements have been concluded and have operated—usually briefly, but in one or two cases over longer periods—in cocoa, coffee, rubber, sugar, tea, tin and wheat. The schemes have provided for various combinations of adjustable export quotas, stockpiling arrangements and reservation of special markets. None has had complete success in preventing large swings in prices, and primary producers, whether of commodities covered by formal agreements or not, have continued to complain of 'unfairly' low prices. This dissatisfaction has, on the initiative of representatives of the developing countries, taken institutional form through the creation of UNCTAD

---

[1] *Proceedings of the Monetary and Economic Conference*, Nos. 1-39, League of Nations, Geneva, 1933.

which, at its meeting in Nairobi in 1976, formulated proposals for action.[1]

This *Paper* will not attempt to examine in detail the history of past attempts to regulate commodity trade by international agreement, except for purposes of illustration. It will seek first to identify the evils widely believed to result from the price structures and fluctuations of international markets in primary commodities and from certain special basic characteristics of those markets. Secondly, it will examine the principles and specific proposals advanced in international discussions to test their inherent practicability and probable efficiency in achieving the desired objectives.

Two objectives: conflicting effects

Two basic aspects of most modern discussions of primary product prices must be emphasised. The first is a strong tendency to assume that the function of prices is to bring about some particular pattern of distribution of income between buyers and sellers and that it is possible to manipulate those prices to achieve a distribution based on ethical principles rather than to achieve a balance between production and consumption. This assumption is more fully discussed later in this *Paper*.

The second aspect is a tendency to be ambiguous about the objective of price manipulation, that is to say, whether it is to reduce the range of price fluctuations *or* to raise average prices above what they would be in a completely free market. The pressure for action has nearly always come from the producers—perhaps because periods of low prices tend to be longer than those of very high prices, but more because a low price for a particular commodity reduces the total income of whole communities specialising in its production, whereas a high price may affect only a single item in the consumer's shopping basket.

An additional reason is that the poorer communities in the world are commonly dependent on primary production—although that is not the same as saying that all primary producers are poor. Consequently, it is in times of depression

---

[1] *Proceedings of the United Nations Conference on Trade and Development: Fourth Session, Nairobi, 5-31 May 1976* (UNCTAD IV), particularly the 'Resolutions and Recommendation on Commodities' in Vol. I: *Report and Annexes,* United Nations, New York, 1977, extracts from which are reprinted below, pp. 24-27.

rather than boom that pressure for intervention is strongest. At such times action to limit fluctuations by cutting out the 'lows' and action to raise average prices are easily confused. Nonetheless, the distinction is vital in considering the mechanics of any regulatory scheme. Some action to protect buyers and sellers from extreme fluctuations is feasible within a free-market system; that is what futures markets are for. The further development of futures markets has received too little attention in discussions of the fluctuation problem. Action to raise and maintain prices *permanently* above their free-market levels involves quite different problems.

(i) *Raising average prices*

Let us take first the objective of raising average prices. What is 'too low' a price for a particular commodity is in any case a subjective judgement, not something capable of calculation on objective economic principles. Judgements are, moreover, apt to be confused by the acceptance of various stereotypes or basic assumptions. It is easy to evoke a picture of poor workers in tropical rice or cane fields, but it does not follow that all producers of rice and sugar have low incomes. There is no reason to think that workers employed in growing rice in the USA or sugar-beet in Europe are any less well-off than the average agricultural worker in those countries, and they are certainly far better-off than the vast numbers of agricultural workers in Asia and Africa. It is true that agricultural producers in most industrialised countries benefit from tariff or other arrangements which enable them to sell at least a large part of their output at prices above those prevailing in international markets. Nonetheless, in evidence given to a House of Lords Committee on commodity policy,[1] Lord Balogh and Professor Peter (now Lord) Bauer found themselves, for once, in agreement in pointing out that a substantial proportion of primary produce supplied to world markets comes from the richer, industrialised countries. Furthermore, within the poorer countries exporting such products, the workers so engaged are commonly less poor

---

[1] *House of Lords Select Committee on Commodity Prices*: Lord Balogh's submission, 'Notes on Commodity Agreements', and oral evidence: Vol. II: *Minutes of Proceedings, Session 1975-76*, HL 165-ii, HMSO, 1977, pp. 45-54; P. T. Bauer and H. Myint, 'Commodity Prices', Appendix 4 to Vol. III: *Minutes of Evidence, 7 July-15 December 1976*, HL 165-iii, HMSO, 1977, pp. 611-14.

than others engaged either in subsistence farming or in producing for a purely local market.

A second important qualification to any plan for an across-the-board increase in primary product prices is that many of the poorer countries, although dependent on exports of specific primary products, are also *importers* of other primary products, including foodstuffs. In particular, most are heavily dependent on imports of oil and have probably suffered more than the industrialised countries from the rise in oil prices imposed by OPEC.

Thirdly, if a fall in prices is due to a good harvest, it may be offset—partially or completely—by higher sales so that fluctuations in prices are not necessarily accompanied by comparable fluctuations in incomes. Where a change in price is due to a change on the demand side or to a fluctuation in the crop prospects of a major producer not shared by *all* producers, however, there may not be any such offset.

Are 'free' markets biassed against primary producers?

Yet another facet of the case put forward for raising the average prices of primary products is the widespread, if not very clearly formulated, belief that 'free' markets as currently operated result in 'unfair' terms of trade between industrial and primary producers and that there is in some way an inherent bias against the latter which only international action by governments can correct.[1] It is not easy to see how this bias is supposed to be created, but one basis for the belief is the claim that prices of industrial products are 'administered' rather than market-determined; that is, at any given moment, the price of a particular make of car or machine tool or computer is laid down by the manufacturer and does not vary from hour to hour like the world price of cotton or coffee or tin.

There is, of course, no terminal market in cars. But that does not mean there is no possibility of negotiating an explicit or concealed discount on the scheduled price (buyers in the domestic market commonly negotiate a discount in the guise of a 'trade-in'); nor does it exclude active competition between rival manufacturers of closely similar, if not identical, models. In the light of their bitter complaints about foreign competition,

[1] Evidence for this belief can be found in the 'Brandt Report', *North-South, op. cit.*, Ch. 9: 'Commodity Trade and Development'.

it is not really credible that manufacturers of automobiles, industrial machinery and so on operate the equivalent of an OPEC agreement. No doubt it is true that work in a factory is, on the average, more remunerative—because it is more productive in the valuation of the world at large—than agricultural work in the poorer countries; whether it is any longer more remunerative as between industrial and agricultural workers in the industrialised countries themselves is less certain.

The remedy is to help the developing world move into the manufacturing field by opening developed markets to them more freely. The identity 'primary-producer=poor man' is certainly not universally valid; bringing aid to the poorest populations requires much more complicated programmes than a simple change in the terms of trade between primary producers and industrial communities—as indeed is recognised in the variety of measures recommended by UNCTAD. The distributional case for an across-the-board rise in primary product prices is at least questionable; its feasibility is discussed later (Section 5).

(ii) *Reducing price fluctuations*

The reduction of wide and rapid price fluctuations appears *prima facie* to be much less open to question as an objective of policy. In recent generations (and perhaps at all times) the prices of primary products have varied more widely within short periods than those of manufactured goods and services. Individual examples of variation have already been given (p. 11).

That prices in 'free' markets fluctuate is clear enough. The examples quoted in the text and illustrated in Chart 1 show the sharp contrasts between highs and lows in particular price ranges. They may, however, exaggerate the swings. Existing information does not normally tell us *how much* of a commodity is sold at the high and low points. The prices reported for the extremes probably relate to comparatively small transactions, so that the range of receipts by producers which properly-weighted figures would show would be distinctly less wide. Moreover, the contrasts shown by recorded prices in organised international markets refer only to a portion of world production. In some foodstuffs most of the

[16]

Chart 1

Price Volatility of Selected Commodities, 1982

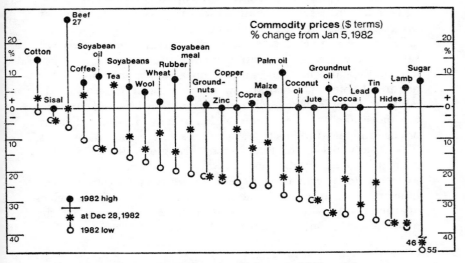

Source: 'Commodities Brief', *The Economist*, 15 January, 1983, p. 80.

output may be sold in purely local markets or be consumed by the producer and his family; and even if markets in many agricultural products are more highly organised, much or all of the production may be sold in restricted markets of one kind or another where prices are only indirectly affected by free-market fluctuations.

Fluctuations and producers

After making allowance for all such qualifications and exceptions, there are, nonetheless, a very substantial number of instances where large groups of producers experience wide variations in the prices of their products and in their incomes. It remains possible, indeed probable, that average prices are still adequate to cover average costs, bearing in mind that millions of people continue to produce the commodities concerned and new producers are continually moving into these lines of production; thus fluctuations are evidently not an absolute deterrent to production. For most of us, however, a higher degree of steadiness of income is worth striving for,

[17]

and it has been frequently argued that variability of income tends to hinder development by reducing the funds people are able or willing to put aside for capital investment.

Yet, as Professor Alasdair MacBean has shown,[1] there is no convincing statistical evidence for this view. Indeed, *a priori,* there is reason to expect that private individuals will save more out of a fluctuating income than out of a steady one because people who can rely on a steady income tend to acquire habits of consumption which absorb most of it. In contrast, people faced with fluctuating prices and incomes are more likely to treat their higher receipts in times of boom as exceptional windfalls to be saved or spent on capital projects. The disadvantages of fluctuations are more likely to affect both private and public expenditure—which can be classified as either long-term consumption or indirect investment—on housing, education and the more elaborate social services characteristic of the more sophisticated economies of the modern world, not the poorest.

Fluctuations and consumers

On the demand side, too, wide fluctuations, if not so potentially catastrophic in their effects, are at least inconvenient. Manufacturers who have to quote prices for their products well in advance may find their profit margins eaten away by large rises in the costs of their raw materials. And, if they have a choice of materials or of sources of energy, they will alternatively suffer loss if their chosen material or energy source rises steeply in price. Or they may lose sales to competitors if a rejected alternative happens to fall in price. The final consumer is equally apt to complain vigorously about rises in the price of items of general consumption such as sugar, coffee or tea, while governments seeking to control inflation and achieve wage-stability will also be sensitive to perceptible fluctuations in prices. There is thus a significant common interest between producers and consumers in avoiding wide fluctuations even though producers will naturally be more concerned to cut out the 'lows' and consumers to avoid the 'highs', and each group's views as to the right 'mean' may diverge substantially.

[1] Alasdair I. MacBean, *Export Instability and Economic Development,* George Allen & Unwin, London, 1966.

[18]

The evils of fluctuating prices may be exaggerated, but evils there indisputably are which it would be good to remove if it could be done without creating ill consequences as side-effects.

Special characteristics of commodity markets

Before considering what might usefully be done to stabilise commodity prices, it is worthwhile asking why primary products (or at least a number of them) are so subject to wide price variations? If they have special characteristics which make them susceptible to wide variability, can anything be done to change or offset those characteristics by more direct means than market manipulation? A brief examination will demonstrate that most primary products do have special characteristics, partly in the physical conditions of their production and partly in the nature of the demand for them.

First, there is the obvious susceptibility of agricultural products to large and, in the main, unpredictable variations in the size of the crop as a result of unfavourable weather conditions, diseases, insect pests, and other natural causes; the sharp fall in Brazilian coffee production a few years ago, for example, was caused by abnormally low temperatures.

Secondly, all the commodities which have been subjected to international control schemes—and most of those included in the UNCTAD list of commodities especially sensitive to price fluctuation—are characterised by a low, or at least slow, responsiveness to price changes either on the supply or on the demand side, or both, as a consequence of dominant technical or social factors.

On the supply side, tea, coffee, cocoa and rubber are all tree crops whose initial planting entails substantial capital costs. After taking up to five years or more to reach maturity, the trees will go on yielding for decades with comparatively low costs of maintenance or of picking or tapping. Cane sugar is also a crop which, once planted, will normally be cut down and allowed to grow up again for a number of years before re-planting; in addition, it requires a formidable investment in processing plant. Sisal and other hard fibres, many fruits and some major sources of vegetable oils are in more or less a similar position. Alongside these are the mineral products where the same basic conditions of heavy long-term capital costs and low current costs prevail. Prices of all these sensitive

[19]

primary products have to fall to very low levels before it ceases to be worthwhile to harvest them from existing trees, canes or mines; and a rise to very high levels must be expected before it is worth investing in new production. Indeed, in certain quite common conditions there may be a 'perverse' reaction to price changes since, in a production unit (a plantation or a mine) working below capacity, the way to reduce costs to cope with lower prices may be to *increase* output. It is not unusual, moreover, for low prices to stimulate the adoption of more efficient techniques which at once reduce costs and raise output.

Primary producer's share in consumers' budgets

There are also factors on the consumption side which make demand slow to react to price changes. The main determinant of demand for, say, tin or rubber is the general state of industrial activity. The cost of raw rubber in the tyres of a motor car or of tin in a can of baked beans is a tiny proportion of the total selling price of the car or the baked beans, so that large variations in the raw material price can be absorbed without affecting consumer demand. Where there is a satisfactory substitute, like synthetic for natural rubber, its cost may set a limit to the price fluctuations; but the use of a substitute often requires a change in manufacturing technique and is not worth undertaking merely because of a short-term rise in price. Even in direct-consumption products sold with little or no intermediate processing, the price paid to the producer is also apt to be a small proportion of the price charged to the final consumer.[1] It so happens that, in many of the commodities liable to particularly wide price fluctuations, the end-products account for only small proportions of total household budgets, and consumers may absorb substantial price variations before demand is affected.

At the same time, demand for commodities which may be classed as semi-luxuries is highly elastic in response to changes in the middle range of incomes; it grows much less rapidly as incomes rise to higher levels. The increase in demand for

[1] The memorandum submitted to the House of Lords Committee by the Institute of Development Studies quotes a ratio of only 11·5 per cent in bananas, which require no processing before sale to the consumer. (*House of Lords Select Committee on Commodity Prices,* Vol. III: *Minutes of Evidence,* Appendix 5, p. 615 (HL 165-iii), HMSO, 1977.)

these commodities in recent times has therefore come largely from countries in the developing world which have been successful in achieving important gains in income per head, rather than from the richer industrialised countries. It may be expected that the developing countries will experience the same decline in the rate of increase of demand as they move to still higher incomes. Thus extrapolation of existing demand trends is dangerous. At the same time, the precise income at which income-elasticity will begin to fall is not easy to predict. Forecasting total demand over any long period remains a risky business.

Supply and demand do respond—but slowly

Thus, for both raw materials and direct-consumption products, demand in the short run is markedly responsive to changes in general economic activity and incomes per head but relatively unresponsive to moderate changes in price. Supply and demand do, nevertheless, respond to price changes in the long run. High prices do prompt people to plant more wheat or coffee or sugar or whatever may be demanded; and low prices do lead at least some producers to think of shifting to alternative crops. On the demand side, markedly higher prices will induce consumers to change their habits—to eat fewer sweets and chocolates (requiring milk, sugar and cocoa), and to switch from coffee to tea or *vice-versa*. The very sharp rise in coffee prices in 1977 undoubtedly led to a reduction in consumption. In manufacturing, high prices for particular raw materials will intensify efforts to economise in their use and may also lead to the substitution of alternatives, either other natural products or synthetics.

The important proposition about sensitivity to price fluctuations is that these reactions are mostly slow. New planting, new investment in processing plants and new mining developments may take years to come into production. Switches by manufacturers to alternative materials may involve changes in production techniques and possibly new machinery, both of which will delay their implementation. Once made, such changes are not lightly reversed; a new plantation or a new manufacturing technique will have a strong tendency towards permanence.

The result of such supply and demand conditions is that

a marked susceptibility to price fluctuations tends to be self-perpetuating. Investment in additional plantings, in new processing plant and in new mines sometimes comes into production long after the boom which stimulated it is over, thereby intensifying the downward pressure on price. A long-term oscillatory effect is thus a natural consequence of the basic physical conditions of production.

Access to markets restricted

One further characteristic of primary product markets is the extent of restrictions which, for some commodities, limit the size of the 'free world market' available on substantially equal terms to all producers. Virtually all the industrialised countries, which constitute the largest buyers, limit access to their markets in differing degrees by systems of support to their own agricultural producers (through tariffs, subsidies, pro-hibitions of imports, quotas, and so on). Such support systems not only often lead to the whole of the domestic market being reserved for national producers. They also generate surpluses, either regularly or occasionally, which are disposed of on the open world market, or in some cases by special deals—often at subsidised prices—that equally reduce the market effectively available to other producers dependent on such open markets for the sale of all or most of their output. Sugar is a notorious example where only about one-fifth of total world output is sold at world market prices, but special arrangements also significantly affect cereals and animal products and, through them, the oil-seeds and vegetable-oil markets. The effect of such special arrangements for large sections of the total world market is to concentrate the impact of fluctuations in demand or supply on the comparatively narrow free market and to widen the range of price fluctuations in it.

THREE: Basic Ideas on International Action

Early attempts to regulate international markets in individual commodities proceeded very much on a trial-and-error basis. As governments replaced producers' organisations as the ultimate controllers, however, efforts were made to formulate general principles for regulation schemes. Two such formulations, adopted internationally, were embodied in the report of the World Monetary and Economic Conference of 1933 and in a resolution adopted by the UNCTAD at its 1976 meeting in Nairobi.

The ideas of 1933

The section of the report of the 1933 Conference concerned with the co-ordination of production and marketing began with the basic statement:

> 'In order to assist in the restoration of world prosperity, it is essential to increase the purchasing power of the producers of primary products by raising the wholesale prices of such products to a reasonable level.'[1]

It went on to lay down the conditions to which any agreements to implement that objective should conform. These conditions, based on a document submitted by the UK Government, were:

'(a) The commodity must be one of great importance for international trade, in which there is such an excess of production or stocks as to call for special concerted action.

(b) The agreement should be comprehensive as regards the commodities to be regulated, that is, it should not be so narrowly drawn as to exclude related or substituted products, if their inclusion is necessary or desirable to ensure the success of the plan.

(c) It should be comprehensive as regards producers, that is:
　　(i) It should in the first instance command a general measure of assent among exporting countries and within these

---

[1] *Journal of the Monetary and Economic Conference*, Issue No. 16, League of Nations, Geneva, 1933, p. 111.

[23]

countries a substantial majority of the producers themselves.

(ii) Where necessary and desirable for the success of the plan, it should provide for the co-operation of non-exporting countries where production is considerable.

(d) It should be fair to all parties, both producers and consumers; it should be designed to secure and maintain a fair and remunerative price level; it should not aim at discriminating against a particular country; and it should as far as possible be worked with the willing co-operation of consuming interests in importing countries who are equally concerned with producers in the maintenance of regular supplies at fair and stable prices.

(e) It should be administratively practicable, that is, the machinery established for its administration should be workable, and the individual governments concerned must have the power and the will to enforce it in their respective territories.

(f) It should be of adequate duration, that is, it should contain provisions for its continuance for such a period as to give assurance to all concerned that its objects can be achieved.

(g) It should be flexible, that is, the plan should be such as to permit of and provide for the prompt and orderly expansion of supply to meet improvement in demand.

(h) Due regard should be had in each country to the desirability of encouraging efficient production.'[1]

So much for the 1933 Conference. Its declaration is critically examined later (pp. 27-28).

The ideas of 1976

The UNCTAD Resolution of 1976 adopted the following 'Integrated Programme for Commodities', which is also analysed later (pp. 27-28, 38, 45-47 and 49-51):

'I. *Objectives*

With a view to improving the terms of trade of developing countries and in order to eliminate the economic imbalance between developed and developing countries, concerted efforts should be made in favour of the developing countries towards expanding and diversifying their trade, improving and diversifying their productive

[1] *Ibid.*

[24]

capacity, improving their productivity and increasing their export earnings, with a view to counteracting the adverse effects of inflation, thereby sustaining real incomes. Accordingly the following objectives are agreed:

1. To achieve stable conditions in commodity trade, including avoidance of excessive price fluctuations, at levels which would:
   (a) be remunerative and just to producers and equitable to consumers;
   (b) take account of world inflation and changes in the world economic and monetary situations;
   (c) promote equilibrium between supply and demand within expanding world commodity trade;

2. To improve and sustain the real income of individual developing countries through increased export earnings, and to protect them from fluctuations in export earnings, especially from commodities;

3. To seek to improve market access and reliability of supply for primary products and the processed products thereof, bearing in mind the needs and interests of developing countries;

4. To diversify production in developing countries, including food production, and to expand processing of primary products in developing countries with a view to promoting their industrialisation and increasing their export earnings;

5. To improve the competitiveness of, and to encourage research and development on the problems of, natural products competing with synthetics and substitutes, and to consider the harmonisation, where appropriate, of the production of synthetics and substitutes in developed countries with the supply of natural products produced in developing countries;

6. To improve market structures in the field of raw materials and commodities of export interest to developing countries;

7. To improve marketing, distribution and transport systems for commodity exports of developing countries, including an increase in their participation in these activities and their earnings from them.

'II. *Commodity Coverage*

The commodity coverage of the Integrated Programme should take into account the interests of developing countries in bananas, bauxite, cocoa, coffee, copper, cotton and cotton yarns, hard fibres and products, iron ore, jute and [jute] products, manganese, meat, phosphates, rubber, sugar, tea, tropical timber, tin, and

[25]

vegetable oils, including olive oil, and oilseeds, among others, it being understood that other products could be included, . . .

'III. *International measures of the Programme*

1. It is agreed that steps will be taken . . . towards the negotiation of a common fund.

2. It is also agreed to take the following measures, to be applied singly or in combination, including action in the context of international commodity arrangements between producers and consumers, in the light of the characteristics and problems of each commodity and the special needs of developing countries:

  (a) Setting up of international commodity stocking arrangements;

  (b) Harmonisation of stocking policies and the setting up of co-ordinated national stocks;

  (c) Establishment of pricing arrangements, in particular negotiated price ranges, which would be periodically reviewed and appropriately revised, taking into account, *inter alia*, movements in prices of imported manufactured goods, exchange rates, production costs and world inflation, and levels of production and consumption;

  (d) Internationally agreed supply management measures, including export quotas and production policies and, where appropriate, multilateral long-term supply and purchase commitments;

  (e) Improvement of procedures for information and consultation on market conditions;

  (f) Improvement and enlargement of compensatory financing facilities for the stabilisation, around a growing trend, of export earnings of developing countries;

  (g) Improvement of market access for the primary and processed products of developing countries through multilateral trade measures in the multilateral trade negotiations, improvement of schemes of generalised preferences and their extension beyond the period originally envisaged, and trade promotion measures;

  (h) International measures to improve the infrastructure and industrial capacity of developing countries, extending from the production of primary commodities to their processing, transport and marketing, as well as to the production of finished manufactured goods, their transport, distribution and exchange, including the establishment of financial, exchange and other institutions for the remunerative management of trade transactions;

[26]

(i) Measures to encourage research and development on the problems of natural products competing with synthetics and consideration of the harmonisation, where appropriate, of the production of synthetics and substitutes in developed countries with the supply of natural products produced in developing countries;

(j) Consideration of special measures for commodities whose problems cannot be adequately solved by stocking and which experience a persistent price decline.

3. The interests of developing importing countries, particularly the least developed and the most seriously affected among them, and those lacking in natural resources, adversely affected by measures under the Integrated Programme, should be protected by means of appropriate differential and remedial measures within the Programme.

4. Special measures, including exemption from financial contributions, should be taken to accommodate the needs of the least developed countries in the Integrated Programme.

5. Efforts on specific measures for reaching arrangements on products, groups of products or sectors which, for various reasons, are not incorporated in the first stage of application of the Integrated Programme should be continued.

6. The application of any of the measures which may concern existing international arrangements on commodities covered by the Integrated Programme would be decided by governments within the commodity organisations concerned.'[1]

So much for the 1976 UNCTAD.

The 1933 formulation of the World Monetary and Economic Conference was concerned only with commodity regulation schemes and not with other measures to improve the welfare of developing countries. It quite clearly envisaged an *increase* in primary product prices as the first objective, with price *stability* following later. It was also much concerned with the *practicability* of schemes.[2]

The 1976 UNCTAD formulation is much broader. It refers to a number of other measures designed to improve the trade and economies of developing countries besides com-

---

[1] *Proceedings of the United Nations Conference on Trade and Development: Fourth Session, Nairobi, 5-31 May 1976,* Vol. I: *Report and Annexes,* '1. Resolutions and Recommendation: Commodities', United Nations, New York, 1977, pp. 6-9, extract from pp. 7-8.

[2] The UK document on which it was based was drafted by civil servants who had been much involved in the detailed working of the tin, rubber and other existing or projected regulation schemes.

modity regulation schemes. But it approaches the issues from a more theoretical standpoint, and shows little explicit recognition of the problems of administration. It is also less clear whether higher or more stable prices should have priority. Whereas the authors of the 1933 document were concerned with a limited and supposedly short-term problem—namely, the peculiarly deep and general depression of commodity prices resulting from the world-wide trade recession of the early 1930s—the thinking behind the UNCTAD resolution is much more general and is concerned with extensive and permanent changes in the mechanisms of world trade. This difference in time-scale has the important consequence that it is more than ever necessary to look at the long-term effects of the control measures envisaged and not to be satisfied with apparent 'successes' in the short term.

The income re-distribution approach of the two declarations

Common to both the 1933 and 1976 declarations, however, is a fundamentally *distributive* approach, that is, a concern with the repercussions of either market fluctuations or regulating devices on the incomes of producers and with undefined ideas of 'fairness' of prices as between buyers and sellers. They both virtually ignore the real character of price changes whose basic function is not to bring about a particular distributive pattern but to balance supply and demand and so allocate resources as closely to the optimum as can reasonably be expected, given the imperfections of human knowledge and the means of communicating such knowledge. The price which balances supply and demand inevitably creates a distributive pattern, but essentially as a by-product or result, not as an objective.

The preoccupation of politicians with income distribution diverts attention from the economic truth that, if markets are not to be allowed to operate so as to bring production and demand into balance, some other mechanism than market prices—ultimately controlled by government and politics—must be established to achieve it. This fundamental alternative must be borne prominently in mind when the practical efficacy and the side-effects of proposals to bring about a 'better' price structure come to be considered (especially if a price is maintained at which producers want to produce more than consumers will buy at that price).

[28]

FOUR: The Indispensable Function of Price

The neglect of the market-clearing function of price changes is reflected in the assumption which seems to underlie so much of the thinking in this field, namely, that both total demand and the pattern of production are fixed irrespective of prices, and therefore that there are no such things as demand and supply curves. Yet the existence of a demand curve is implicit in the advocacy of some form of quota restriction scheme, since the object of restricting offers to the market is to push up the price. But even that is glossed over in schemes, now more frequently advocated, which put restriction in a secondary role. Supply curves are even less regarded.

It was perhaps not unreasonable in 1933 to think of a rigid pattern of demand and potential supply over a limited period, and of regulation agreements as *limited*-term devices to deal once and for all with an exceptional period of depression. The commodities then most clearly in mind were those, such as rubber and tin, where potential productive capacity was fixed for a significant period by the size of existing plantations or established mines and concentrated in a handful of countries, while consumption, if not fixed absolutely, was dependent on factors outside the rubber or tin markets—above all by world industrial activity. It is quite unjustified to extend the assumption of a fixed market to a permanent 'new order' of international trade designed to cover for an unlimited period a much wider range of commodities with very different and frequently much more flexible technical bases of production, including, for example, the considerable complex of products grouped together as 'vegetable oils and oil seeds'.

Changes in sources of supply

The history of the production of the sensitive commodities shows clearly how much the pattern can change, if not in a year or two, at least over a few decades. A few examples will illustrate the argument. For a brief period before 1912 rubber production was almost a monopoly of Brazil; by 1938, of total world exports of 889,000 tons, Malaya contributed 40 per cent and Indonesia 34 per cent. In 1975 estimated world production had grown to nearly 13·67 million tons but synthetic rubber contributed 68 per cent of the total, while Malayan and Indonesian natural rubber accounted for only about 12 and 7 per cent respectively.[1]

In 1938 world production of coffee was estimated at about 2 million tons, with Brazil contributing 65 per cent, other Latin American countries about 22½ per cent and African countries 12½ per cent. In the seven years from 1973-4 to 1979-80 world production averaged about 4·35 million tons a year, of which Brazil contributed 27 per cent, other Latin American countries about 30 per cent and Africa about 25 per cent.[2]

Brazil, which was of minor importance in the world sugar market before World War II, has become the largest producer of cane sugar in the world, and in 1980 surpassed Russia as a producer of any type of sugar. Russia itself, a significant exporter before 1914, has become a large importer, with net imports averaging 4 million tons a year between 1975 and 1980 and approaching 5 million tons in 1980. Indonesia, second only to Cuba as an exporter to the world market in the 1930s, now produces less than its internal requirements and had net imports averaging over 450,000 tons a year during the period 1977-80. Thailand, formerly a regular importer on a small scale, had average exports of over 1·1 million tons over the same period. Finally, the EEC has increased its net exports from less than 1 million tons in 1977 to a reported 5 million tons a year today. These figures may be set against total world net exports in 1980 of about 23 million tons and total world output of centrifugal (factory) sugar of about 84 million tons.

These examples illustrate that the pattern of production of primary products is not fixed in a way which can be the basis of a simple plan. It is constantly, and often rapidly, changing. Without the possibilities for such change, the growth of economic activity essential to the improvement of

---

[1] These and other commodity statistics are based on figures in the *Commodity Year Book, 1981,* published by the Commodity Research Bureau, Inc., New York.

[2] A seven-year average is taken in order not to exaggerate the effect of the catastrophic drop in Brazil's coffee production in 1977 as a result of extraordinary weather conditions.

The Price of Stability . . . ?

SIR SYDNEY CAINE

1. Wide fluctuations in primary product prices have caused concern for many years.

2. The so-called 'North-South' debate has further encouraged proposals to restrict market forces in favour of various types of government intervention.

3. The ancestry of such proposals can be traced back to the 1976 UNCTAD Conference and the World Economic Conference of 1933.

4. Even now, however, there is no agreement about the aims of intervention by governments.

5. Some confuse smoothing out fluctuations in prices with raising the average level of prices.

6. Others set aside the role of price in bringing production and consumption into balance, and try to use regulation by means of quotas, stockpiling, compensation schemes, etc. to promote a more equal (international) distribution of incomes.

7. An alternative approach consists of measures to improve the functioning of the market.

8. These would include steps to increase primary producers' access to markets at present protected by industrialised countries.

9. Improvements should be made to the flow of information about market trends and production plans.

10. A new scheme is suggested for an international agency to act as a broker in arranging long-term contracts.

Hobart Paper 97 is published (price £1·50) by

THE INSTITUTE OF ECONOMIC AFFAIRS
2 Lord North Street, Westminster
London SW1P 3LB   Telephone: 01-799 3745

IEA PUBLICATIONS

Subscription Service

An annual subscription is the most convenient way to obtain our publications. Every title we produce in all our regular series will be sent to you immediately on publication and without further charge, representing a substantial saving.

Subscription rates*

Britain: £15.00 p.a. including postage.

£14.00 p.a. if paid by Banker's Order.

£10.00 p.a. teachers and students who pay *personally.*

Europe and South America: £20 or equivalent.

Other countries: Rates on application. In most countries subscriptions are handled by local agents.

*These rates are *not* available to companies or to institutions.

To: The Treasurer, Institute of Economic Affairs,
2 Lord North Street,
Westminster, London SW1P 3LB.

I should like to subscribe beginning ....

I enclose a cheque/postal order for:

☐ £15.00

☐ Please send me a Banker's Order form

☐ Please send me an Invoice

☐ £10.00 [I am a teacher/student at..]

Name ....

Address ....

....

Signed .... Date ....

HP97

conditions in the developing world would be impossible. Moreover, the changes have taken place in the context, and in response to the stimulus, of actively functioning world markets. One of the most important questions to ask about any proposal to regulate those markets, or substitute an entirely new international economic order, is: How will it accommodate the continuation of such change and economic growth?

What solutions?

It is time to turn from these brief reminders of the special features of primary product markets to an examination of the measures proposed to remedy their alleged defects. In this *Paper,* attention is concentrated on measures which are of general concern, in the sense that they are designed to exert a powerful influence on world markets in primary commodities or to replace them by some other general system. Before examining such schemes in more detail, other measures should be noted which have been used or proposed to mitigate the effects on particular groups of producers of wide fluctuations in the world prices of commodities. These are:

(a) National marketing boards, themselves selling at world prices, but buying from individual producers at prices in some way averaged over the years so as to give them steadier incomes;

(b) Bulk-purchase agreements between individual countries under which prices are fixed for a term of years or at least varied less frequently and less violently than world market prices;

(c) Various forms of compensation schemes under which individual countries or producers receive compensation for loss of earnings due to falls in export prices.

(a) *Marketing boards*

Marketing boards were at one time much favoured as a means of stabilising producers' incomes. More recently they seem to have lost support, possibly because they have often been used to divert the 'excess' proceeds of sales in times of high prices to government funds rather than to reserves for maintaining prices in subsequent slumps, and partly perhaps because of the difficulty of distinguishing secular trends in prices from

[31]

temporary fluctuations in the price curve for the purposes of averaging, especially in an inflationary world. Inflation must also make less attractive the idea of accumulating reserve funds whose real value can be expected to decline.

(b) *Bulk purchase agreements*

Bulk-purchase agreements, such as the Commonwealth Sugar Agreement, the Lomé Convention, and various agreements between the centrally-planned countries, have undoubtedly been beneficial to the individual groups of producers involved, but at the expense of excluded producers and of would-be, new or developing producers. On balance, they have *widened* the range of price fluctuation in open world markets by narrowing the market available to all and sundry.

(c) *Compensation schemes*

Compensation schemes which are in operation or have been proposed may be divided into two categories:

(i) those designed to offset at least part of a decline in the export earnings of *national units,* including a decline resulting from lower export prices, crop failures, or other factors beyond the exporting country's control; and

(ii) those designed to compensate, partly or wholly, *individual producers* who suffer loss of income from such causes.

Two schemes of the first type are currently in operation. The EEC's Lomé Convention[1] with 63 developing countries incorporates an export earnings stabilisation scheme, known as Stabex. Originally, Stabex applied to only 12 agricultural raw materials (plus iron ore) but has subsequently been expanded to cover 44 commodities. A special arrangement for minerals, known as Sysmin, was added in 1980. Through the Stabex scheme, the EEC provides aid (in the form of grants and cheap loans) to the developing-country signatories of the

[1] The first Lomé Convention (which was the successor to the Yaoundé Convention dating back to 1963) was signed in 1975 between the EEC and a large number of developing countries—known as the African, Caribbean and Pacific states, or ACPs—which at one time had been colonies of member states of the newly-enlarged EEC. It provided for the EEC to extend to the developing country signatories favourable treatment in aid and trade, and it established institutions for consultation and negotiation. It was renewed in 1979 (Lomé II), by which time 63 developing countries had become adherents.

Lomé Convention to make up their losses in export earnings for any of the 44 commodities. It is, however, subject to a variety of conditions—not least that it applies only to exports to the EEC. It is also subject to a financial limit; its budget for 1980-85 was originally set at approximately $520 million. More recently, following the sharp fall in commodity prices, there have been complaints about its inadequacy. In 1981 it ran seriously short of cash and the EEC agreed to double its resources. Despite that increase, it was reported as being sufficient to meet no more than half the claims made on it that year. Moreover, almost 80 per cent of all payments were for just two products: coffee and groundnuts. The gap between the authorised provision and the claims no doubt reflects the natural reluctance of the EEC members to increase their contributions to Stabex when they themselves have also been suffering from the general trade recession.

The second scheme of the first type is the IMF's Compensatory Financing Facility which was designed to extend the Fund's financial support to its member countries—particularly primary commodity exporting countries—encountering balance-of-payments difficulties caused by shortfalls in their export proceeds. A member may draw up to 100 per cent of its Fund quota to compensate for a shortfall, provided the Fund is satisfied the shortfall is temporary and largely attributable to circumstances beyond the member's control. Although established in 1963, this facility was originally hedged with stringent conditions and the total drawings on it amounted to only $1·25 billion during the 12 years to 1975. In that year the conditions were significantly liberalised and drawings have since increased sharply. At 30 April 1982, total outstanding drawings amounted to approximately $16·25 billion.

A compensation scheme of the second kind, linked directly to producers' needs and operating on an insurance basis, was proposed some years ago by Professor P. T. (now Lord) Bauer and Professor Basil Yamey,[1] but has not been implemented. Its adoption could even out at least some market fluctuations for producers taking advantage of it—though it would be a matter for individual discretion how much it was used. The Bauer-Yamey plan was concerned only with

---

[1] 'Organised Commodity Stabilisation with Voluntary Participation', *Oxford Economic Papers*, March 1964, reprinted in P. T. Bauer and B. S. Yamey, *Markets, Market Control and Marketing Reform*, Weidenfeld and Nicolson, London, 1968.

downward fluctuations, but there is no reason in principle why there should not be a complementary insurance scheme for *consumers* desiring cover against *upward* movements.

(d) *International schemes of regulation*

More general schemes aimed in principle at influencing the world market as a whole and serving the interests of all producers may be grouped into three categories:

(i) Regulation of production or export with the object of maintaining an agreed price or price range;

(ii) Stockpiling with the same object of holding price variations within an explicit or tacitly-understood range (whether operating automatically as in the scheme proposed by Grondona[1] or on a discretionary basis as in the tin stockpile agreement); and

(iii) Measures to improve the working of world markets, entailing not only the widening of such markets by reducing the reservations of domestic markets referred to above (p. 22), but a variety of other measures not normally much discussed at international conferences. These would include the improvement of information about development plans, factors affecting either supply or demand in the future, and the development of long-term deals and other forms of dealings in futures.[2]

---

[1] L. St. Clare Grondona, *Utilizing World Abundance,* George Allen and Unwin, London, 1958; also his submissions and evidence to the House of Lords Select Committee on Commodity Prices, Vol. II: *Minutes of Proceedings, Session 1975-76,* and *Minutes of Evidence*, HL 165-ii, HMSO, 1977. As outlined in the introductory chapter of his book, the Grondona scheme in essence depended on the establishment of an autonomous Price Stabilising Corporation (PSC) financed by government-guaranteed bonds, which would hold stocks of basic commodities such as 'grain, textile raw materials, rubber, the industrial metals, and many other products in crude or early-processed form' (p. 13). Each commodity would have its own 'valorising index' (based on its minimum value in, say, sterling) and the PSC would stand ready to buy stocks at 10 per cent below its index value and sell on demand at 10 per cent above index. The PSC would never enter the market, which would continue to function as normally, but could operate 'only on the initiative, first, of sellers and, then, of buyers—neither having recourse to it excepting as a last resort' (p. 14). It would not therefore 'acquire stocks until there was a substantial decline in market prices of the commodities concerned' (p. 15). The scheme was set out 'in all its detailed workings' in the main body of the book.

[2] Futures are contracts entered into through an organised commodity exchange for the purchase or sale of specified quantities of a commodity at a specified

[Continued opposite]

Given the basic function of the market as a mechanism for balancing demand and supply and as a guide to the allocation of resources, the different relationships to the market of these three types of measures are significant. The measures in the third group all accept the market mechanism but aim to make it more generally operative and/or more efficient. The second type of scheme, based on the acquisition and subsequent release of stocks, allows the market to function reasonably normally between its lowest buying price and highest selling price but must tend to put a brake on market reactions and on the repercussions on supply and demand as prices get near to the crucial buying or selling points. The precise impact of a scheme of this kind must depend on how far its operating points are publicly known. To some degree, however, its operation must distort price movements within this price range and, in general, delay supply and demand decisions consequent upon price changes. The extent of the price distortions and the delay in reactions naturally depend on both the extent of the financial resources available to any such scheme and the range within which it operates—and especially on how far that range is correctly related to the average price which would have prevailed in the absence of intervention.

The first type of scheme, imposing quotas on production or export, aims most clearly to replace the market by other mechanisms to discharge its basic functions. Its success depends on its capacity to enforce imposed levels of output over a substantial part of production. This need not be quite all-inclusive since some margin of unrestricted production responding normally to prices can be tolerated. The administrative problems of enforcing quotas and the practical and psychological problems created by the existence of a margin of unrestricted production depend on how far, if at all, the target price or price range of the scheme exceeds what would have been the average price in a free market, and on what incentive its operations offer to unregulated producers to increase their output and thereby necessitate even tighter

price, delivery to be made at a fixed future date. Commonly such contracts are met not by the delivery of the actual commodity but by a financial settlement determined by the difference between the contract price and the price prevailing at the date of its maturity. Trades are guaranteed by a clearing house and deposits or 'margin' are required to ensure completion of the contracts.

control over the production of the regulated producers.

Before evaluating the various measures proposed for raising average prices or mitigating fluctuations or offsetting the effects of fluctuations, we will briefly examine the experience of some of the regulation schemes which have operated with some semblance of success.

Past experience: the inter-war period

In the inter-war period quota regulation was the device most commonly favoured in the rubber, tea, tin and sugar schemes, backed in tin by stockpiling arrangements. It was assumed that a demand curve existed and that a 'satisfactory' price would be established by an appropriate restriction of supply. The exact shape of the demand curve was, of course, not known (and no doubt varied with economic activity); nor was the 'satisfactory' price defined initially. In practice, the councils which operated the schemes were always feeling their way towards a tolerable balance between higher prices and a not-too-burdensome restriction of production. In any one scheme there were differences of opinion between producer groups about what constituted 'satisfactory' prices and how much was worth paying through the restriction of output. Decisions were therefore nearly always negotiated compromises between different viewpoints and not ideal for any one group.

The acceptability of restrictions on output was affected by both administrative and social factors. In tin, for instance, the administrative difficulties of control were lessened by the comparatively large size of most of the units of production. There were nonetheless significant differences in the capacity of governments to exercise effective control—which Malaya and Indonesia, for example, achieved, but Bolivia and Thailand did not. Equally, there were differences in the social implications; in Malaya, for instance, unemployment created by restriction could at least be reduced by ceasing to recruit labour from China and even to make some repatriation. In Bolivia, where all the labour was indigenous and alternative opportunities for work almost non-existent, unemployment was both socially and politically a much more serious matter.

Administrative control

Similar variations existed in the conditions affecting the restriction of rubber production. It was easiest to enforce in the plantations of Malaya and Ceylon, where administrative difficulties were minimised by the existence of large, well-controlled units and efficient, honest government, while social consequences were lessened, as in Malayan tin, by the reliance on a largely immigrant workforce (in this instance, Indian) whose numbers could be reduced by the suspension of recruitment to replace wastage or by repatriation. Administrative control of the European-owned plantations in Indonesia was also not too difficult, though the social consequences of unemployment were more severe because the labour force was mainly indigenous. In addition, Indonesia, and to a lesser extent Malaya, had to cope with a substantial output of rubber from smallholdings, involving large numbers of small production units. Malaya, whose proportion of smallholding production was lower, was able to impose sufficiently effective control, but the problem of direct administrative control was never solved in Indonesia. Instead, its Government was obliged to resort to a special tax on exports of 'native' or smallholder rubber, thereby reducing the net price to the producer and in effect coming close to re-establishing the market mechanism for the small producers and the price discouragement which the international regulation scheme had been designed to bring to an end.

New entrants

The international market for rubber, tin and tea was dominated by no more than half-a-dozen producing countries and it was not thought necessary to work out quota systems covering every producer in the world. Nonetheless, problems developed around potential new or growing producers. They would doubtless have had to be provided for in some way if the systems of export control had continued. The market for rubber was, of course, transformed by the development, much accelerated by wartime needs, of synthetic rubber in the USA and elsewhere, and the natural rubber regulation scheme was not revived after World War II.

In 1937 and subsequently, an attempt was made to work out a fully comprehensive world scheme of quotas for sugar. After World War II, an agreed relationship for adjusting quotas to prices was introduced under which permitted quotas of exports to the free world market changed automatically as the market price rose or fell by prescribed amounts above or below a standard figure. For a variety of reasons none of the successive versions of the International Sugar Agreement has remained in operation for long enough to test the effectiveness of these provisions.

Basic problems of administration

These schemes for regulating quotas did at least recognise that, if market forces were not allowed to guide the adjustments in production required to meet changes in demand, other means had to be devised. They clearly illustrate the practical problems of administering any scheme based on the control of production.

The problems are numerous. Very little, for instance, has been said in recent discussions of regulation schemes about the fixing and periodical revision of quotas; the UNCTAD resolution of 1976 is silent on this all-important aspect. In past experience, quota fixing has perhaps been easiest in certain minerals, the production of which (for purely physical reasons) is concentrated in a relatively small number of areas. Diamonds are the best example of long-continued success in maintaining prices—under a control exercised, however, by commercial interests and not by governments. The inter-war history of the tin and rubber schemes shows how success could be achieved briefly if a few countries control by far the larger part of total production. Yet even with those schemes there was never full and permanent agreement about quotas. The problem becomes progressively worse the more countries there are involved and the longer a regulation scheme continues.

Large changes in the balance of production have taken place in the last few decades and there is no reason to suppose that similar changes will not take place as, or more, quickly in the future. The task of adjusting export or production quotas to take account of potential changes on a scale similar to those of the past is daunting, to say the least.

FIVE: More Recent Developments

Since World War II there have been a number of attempts to establish regulation schemes for commodities such as sugar (already mentioned), cocoa, coffee, copper, tin and other primary products. Following the UNCTAD Resolution of 1976, new agreements have been signed covering cocoa, coffee, rubber, sugar, tin and jute. Not all, however, are in effective operation.

The most recent agreements, though negotiated within the context of the UNCTAD policy declarations, vary in the emphasis they place on buffer-stock operations on the one side, or export quotas on the other, although the general tendency appears to be to rely increasingly on buffer-stock operations. The cocoa scheme is basically a buffer-stock arrangement with no more than imprecise references to export controls by individual signatories and 'other measures' to be initiated by the Cocoa Council. Rubber, similarly, hinges on buffer-stock operations allied to agreed prices. For tin, the emphasis is on stockpiling, with floor and ceiling prices laid down, but subject to variation by the Tin Council and backed up, if necessary, by export controls based on recent export performance. The latest sugar agreement follows earlier models in basing control on pre-determined quotas varied in response to precisely-defined price changes, reliance on stock operations being confined to a provision for the accumulation of a reserve stock to be used to meet an unexpected excess of demand over supply. The coffee agreement similarly relies on export quotas allied to prescribed prices— with, however, provisions for those prices to be adjusted to take account of inflation and for the Coffee Council to ascertain stocks and to study the feasibility of some kind of policy related to stocks. A scheme has been agreed for jute but is not yet in operation because essential financial support from the Common Fund is not available.

None of these schemes has been in effective operation for long enough to allow an assessment of their efficacy as permanent instruments of control. Judging from newspaper

[39]

reports, all seem to have encountered difficulties of coverage or administration. The cocoa agreement, for instance, does not cover either the largest producer (the Ivory Coast) or the largest consumer (the USA); and the scheme appears to have run into early difficulties in financing its obligations to buy cocoa at the prevailing market price. In other schemes, where the governing council has discretion in its purchase or sale operations, differences have been reported between the exporting and importing members. In coffee and tin, the markets seem to have been affected more by the marketing policies of individual member countries than by decisions of the relevant council.

Problems of operation

It seems clear that no reliable pattern of regulation has yet emerged. The inter-war regulation schemes recognised that if market forces were not allowed to guide the adjustments in production required to meet changes in the balance of supply and demand, other means must be devised. That recognition is implicit, though less precisely provided for, in the most recent agreements. But experience, both in the inter-war years and since, clearly illustrates the practical problems of administering any scheme to control production or export. The problems include the fixing and periodical review of quotas (especially to take account of new producers, an aspect which is rarely provided for); the enforcement of such quotas; and the repercussions both on and of the development of competing products.

Solutions have naturally been easiest to find when a high percentage of production is under the control of a small number of producers and the operation is more like that of a producers' cartel than a mutual agreement between producers and consumers. The most successful cartel, no doubt, is that for diamonds, where a very large proportion of world output is under the control of a single operator, and for some other minerals—aluminium, tin and copper, for example—where a concentration of production in a limited number of operators has at times made control effective. But, as the history of OPEC's attempt to control world oil prices on behalf of producer interests illustrates, such control is vulnerable in the longer run both to disagreements within the controlling group and to the competition incurred from entirely new production by sources outside the initial group.

The problems of controlling quotas become progressively more difficult as the number of producing countries increases, and the longer the control has to last. As has already been seen (pp. 29-30), large changes in the balance of production of many commodities have taken place in the last four or five decades and there is no reason to suppose that similar changes will not take place in the future. The task of adjusting export or production quotas to take account of such changes is daunting.

Additional difficulties must arise where a commodity is wholly or largely interchangeable with others; there could be little hope of achieving a regulation agreement covering, for example, the vastly variegated range of oils and oil seeds.

The experience of the inter-war years also showed the dfficulty of enforcing quotas when a multitude of small-scale producers are involved, as with rubber in the (then) Netherlands East Indies. Enforcement is intimately linked with the price level a regulation scheme is aiming to maintain. By definition, as it were, a system of quota regulation means that a significant number of producers are being prevented from selling produce they would still find it worthwhile to sell even at low prices; the higher the price, the more producers will find themselves in that position and the stronger will be the temptation for governments as well as individuals to evade the controls. The pressure to evade the rules and break the agreement is all the stronger when, as can happen with many primary products (particularly tree and other perennial crops and minerals), marginal costs are below average costs, and when excess productive capacity exists and there are no costs of new planting or opening up of new mines.

The last practical problem mentioned was that of substitutes. The regulation of natural rubber stimulated the development of the synthetic substitute. Its success was a main reason for the decision not to revive the regulation scheme after World War II. Other natural products which are threatened by existing or potential synthetic substitutes include cotton and wool (by man-made fibres), sugar (by cyclamates and other artificial sweeteners), and various metals (in some uses, at least, by plastics).

All these difficulties thus indicate that the prospect of effective enforcement of any comprehensive worldwide scheme

[41]

to control export or production for more than a very short time appears poor, even for commodities whose production is concentrated in a few countries, and virtually hopeless where production is widely scattered. The prospect must be even poorer if, and to the extent that, the aim of regulation is to raise average prices and not merely reduce fluctuations. Even if it could be achieved, such a raising of primary product prices would be an inefficient and costly way of helping the poorest communities of the world. Moreover, if it depends on restricting output, and therefore on discouraging newcomers to the industry, regulation is likely to add to rather than reduce the disadvantages of the least developed peoples.

Stockpiling

It is probably a realisation of these problems that has led to more emphasis being placed in recent discussions on the second type of measures, those designed to influence prices by stock operations. Such measures have the attraction that they do not, at any rate initially, depend on administrative action by a large number of governments—as production controls must. They can be administered by a single—presumably expert—body. Given adequate financial resources and a correct judgement about the international equilibrium price around which fluctuations may be allowed to take place, a buffer stock scheme can, in principle, hold prices within an agreed range by buying in all production surplus to effective demand at the low point of the price range and by selling from stock to meet any demand in excess of current offerings by producers at the high point. The practical problems which arise concern:

(a) The determination of the price range;

(b) The extent to which the commodity can conveniently be stored over longish periods, and the cost of such storage;

(c) The resources likely to be required to carry out the obligation to buy in surpluses at the bottom end of the price range;

(d) The stocks which ought to be held in reserve at the top end to check runaway rises in price.

[42]

The modern world of inflation and unstable currencies gives rise to two subsidiary, but potentially crucial, questions:

(a) In what currency or combination of currencies should any price parameters be expressed?

(b) How should inflation generally be taken into account?

These questions are obviously connected. As to the first, although the figures may be a matter of dispute, it might not be too difficult to decide in principle that prices should be expressed in a named currency (or a group of currencies) corrected periodically to allow for changes in both its internal purchasing power and its average exchange value against other major currencies. In the light of the considerable changes in the relative standing of major currencies over the last two decades, however, the choice of a particular currency might soon become out of date. The answer to the second question may be harder to find; just how is it possible to measure general inflation on the scale that has taken place over the last decade?

No automatic formula can be put forward for fixing the basic price range. It must be a matter of judgement in the light of recent history and whatever developments in both supply and demand can be foreseen. Even the finest experts can be wrong about future prices. In November 1956, during a review of the International Sugar Agreement, there was a long discussion about the prices (starting at a little over 3 cents per pound) at which quota increases might be authorised. A proposal that all controls should be suspended if prices rose above 4 cents was accepted with no discussion because the experts 'knew' the price would not rise to that height. Two days later the Anglo-French attack on Suez began and the price shot up to over 5 cents.

That incident was a failure to foresee a *rise* in price. The bigger danger in the current climate of discussion of commodity policy must be that, in the apparent interests of primary producers, the price range will be pitched too high. Supposing that danger to be avoided, there remains the issue of deciding the width of the target price range (the spread between the stockpiles' buying and selling points). The effect of stock operations must be to put a brake on price movements in the vicinity of the buying and selling points and so to delay the adjustments in production and consumption required to correct the market imbalance which led to the downward or upward pressure on prices.

High prices ...

Prima facie, it seems likely that a stockpiling scheme will be more effective in preventing downward movements in prices. The ability of the operating authority to buy up surpluses depends on its financial resources and on the availability of suitable storage facilities, both of which can be enlarged if the case for doing so is strong enough, although the cost may ultimately cause the operations to be terminated. On the other hand, its ability to release stocks to meet a market shortage depends on the physical availability of stocks at that time and nothing can create them if they do not exist. The charts of market prices in recent decades suggest that the more sensational price movements have been upward swings due to such specific causes as widespread harvest failures, freak weather conditions (as with coffee in 1976), and political and military instability (the Korean war and fears of its expansion in 1951, Suez in 1956, and later outbreaks of war in the Middle East). None of these occurrences is likely to be easy to foresee long before the event.

Downward price movements are more apt to be due to a general depression of world economic activity, and (except when they are a reaction to price rises caused by temporary conditions) are generally both less sharp and more sustained than upward movements. Unless the exceptional factors causing sharp upward movements occur when the operating authority has very large stocks—perhaps because they arise at the end of a long depression during which the authority has been buying heavily—a stockpiling scheme would probably be a poor defence against occasional very high prices. One factor which would certainly have some importance in such circumstances, but which cannot be precisely estimated, is the likelihood of a reduction in commercial stocks as a result of its being known that large stocks were in the hands of the public authority which it would release if an acute market shortage developed.

[44]

. . . and low prices

How much more successful is a stockholding authority likely to be in coping with a long period of *low* prices? The answer obviously depends on the size of the financial resources available to the scheme. Those resources cannot be infinite; while the removal of market pressures will only perpetuate the basic imbalance between supply and demand, thus requiring more and more surpluses to be bought in by the stockpile. The aim of significantly enlarging the resources available to support a particular commodity through the UNCTAD Common Fund is based on the hope that the Fund will not find itself faced with depressed prices in all relevant commodities at the same time. If, however, the depression is due to a low level of economic activity in consuming countries—as seems likely for both historical and *a priori* reasons—it is probable that most, if not all, primary products will be affected, and the advantages of averaging the burden of support will therefore be small. Eventually, the financial resources will be exhausted and additions to stock will have to cease.

The option available to national support programmes of selling surpluses on a wider market at lower prices (as with various European agricultural products) is obviously not open to a worldwide support scheme. 'Give-away' programmes, such as those resorted to by the USA, have a certain appeal if applied to bulk foodstuffs which could be made available to poor communities or areas temporarily hit by famine; but they are hardly suitable for raw materials or semi-luxuries like coffee, cocoa and tea. Even the free distribution of bulk foods on large scale would have disturbing effects on local markets and local production unless administered with a refinement and care which it is not reasonable to expect.

In the last resort, therefore, any system of price support based on stock operations must—as the history of the tin stockpile shows—be buttressed by quota regulation of production, the drawbacks of which have already been discussed (pp. 34-36). The only sure ways to avoid problems of production control would be to fix the minimum buying price deliberately low and/or place a limit on the amount of stock which could be bought, and thereafter allow prices to fall. Either method would render any scheme much less attractive from the producer angle.

On a realistic view, the most that can probably be expected

from a scheme based on stock operations is that it would delay price rises or falls outside the effective limits of its chosen price range; and it might wholly prevent such movements if they were the consequence only of *short*-term influences. Unless supported by physical controls on production, such a scheme would probably not be able to prevent price rises resulting from acute actual or apprehended shortage, or to maintain prices in a period of long-continued depression. Moreover, delaying appropriate reactions, i.e. increasing or reducing production and reducing or increasing demand, might mean that the price changes required to bring about those reactions would ultimately be more extreme or more prolonged than otherwise.

The Common Fund

Given the tendency to rely increasingly on buffer-stock techniques in commodity agreements, it is inevitable that the financing of such operations should emerge as a critical factor in their development. While it is normally expected that producers of the commodity, and usually consumers as well, should contribute to that financing, the size of the resources required for a scheme to be able to buy up and hold large quantities of the commodity in order to maintain prices in a depression makes additional finance essential in most, if not all, cases. The Common Fund, agreed to in principle in 1977, is intended to provide access to additional finance for individual commodity schemes. Although the scope eventually determined for it was substantially more limited than envisaged in the propoals of the UNCTAD secretariat, it offered the prospect of significant financial support.

So far, however, it has not lived up even to the lower expectations induced by the agreement in principle reached in 1977. The Fund cannot come into operation until two-thirds of the signatories (about 70 countries) have ratified the agreement. To date, only about 40 have done so. They include the UK and a number of industrialised countries, but other major potential contributors—above all the USA—have failed to ratify. At present, therefore, the Common Fund is unable to help bring into effective operation a number of potentially important agreements, including the recent agreement on jute (p. 39).

- ANNOUNCING A MAJOR NEW TITLE FROM METHUEN -

EQUALITY, THE THIRD WORLD AND ECONOMIC DELUSION

—————P. T. BAUER—————

In this controversial book Professor Bauer directly
challenges some of the most influential ideas of
contemporary economics. Confronting these accepted
ideas with the results of straightforward observation,
reflection and analysis, he argues that many staples
of economic debate and policy at home and abroad are
demonstrably invalid.

The topics discussed fall under three broad headings
– equality, the West and the Third World and the state
of contemporary economics. In addition to a detailed
and stimulating section on foreign aid there is an
extremely important essay on population growth in which
Bauer refutes the widely held view that the recent rapid
increase in population has hindered economic and social
development. In his discussion of these and other issues,
for instance the dollar problem, Bauer raises many thought-
provoking questions which should be of interest and
accessible to students and those unfamiliar with economic
jargon.

P T Bauer is Professor of Economics at the London School
of Economics and Political Science.

300 pages
Paperback: 0 416 34230 2: £5.95

'Peter Bauer is one of the most distinguished development economists in the world, and undoubtedly the foremost conservative one .... This book ... gives an excellent account of his main theses on development policy and international relations. It also presents his approach to economic equality and inequality in general, and places his discussions of development against the background of some of the broadest issues of political economy ...."The Population Explosion: Myths and Realities" is probably the most perceptive and clear-headed analysis of this confusing problem that can be found in the literature. He also makes a powerful critique of "commodity stabilization arrangements" .... This is an extremely important work. It applies and extends a view that is widely held .... The book is both illuminating and provocative. The reader is forced to ask himself if he accepts Bauer's reasoning and if not, why not.'
Amartya Sen, The New York Review of Books

ORDER FORM

Sender's Name ....

Address ....

....

Signature .... Date ....

I wish to order ..... copy/ies of Equality, the Third World and Economic Delusion @ £6.60 (includes post and packing)

I enclose a cheque payable to: Alternative Bookshop for

£ ......

Please send your cheque with order form to:
Alternative Bookshop, 3 Langley Court, Covent Garden, London WC2

In any event, too much should not be expected of the Common Fund. In the first place, the total contributions it will receive if all potential members eventually ratify the agreement will be only $750 million—compared with the estimated $9,000 million required to absorb existing excess supplies.[1]

This disparity between the finance potentially available to the Common Fund and the demands upon it which are already foreseen simply illustrates the fundamental difficulty of all stockpiling schemes. Finance to buy up surpluses in times of depressed prices is no doubt a prerequisite for success; but it is by no means a certain guarantee. If the arguments set out in this *Paper* about the problems of stockpiling schemes are correct, no financial fund which it is reasonable to envisage will be adequate to meet the costs in the long run of endeavouring to maintain prices above market-clearing levels by purchases for stock.

[1] *Financial Times*, 26 January 1983.

SIX: The Alternative: Improving the Market

The third category of measures consists of those designed not to control or replace market forces but to improve the functioning of the market.

Let us recall the special characteristics of world markets for the sensitive primary commodities which appear to make their prices particularly liable to wide fluctuations. Fundamentally, many of the commodities have low elasticities both of supply and demand. Supply is inelastic (in the short run) because of long production cycles and high fixed specific investment in plantations, mines or processing plant. Demand is inelastic for most raw materials either because their price is only a small element in the cost of the final products in which they are embodied, or (as with some of the most sensitive agricultural products) because they are semi-luxuries forming only a small proportion of personal budgets. The reaction of supply to low prices is particularly slow because marginal costs are normally below average costs, so that production may remain profitable until a point is reached where additional output requires further investment in fixed capital. For some agricultural products, moreover, the available world market is artificially restricted by the reservation by governments of large parts of the total world market to national or other favoured producers.

Market-based improvements: access, information, contracts

Can anything be done to reduce the impact of these characteristics and to make the market work more smoothly? Three lines of approach suggest themselves. First, world markets could be widened by reducing the reservation of special parts of them—above all by curtailing the agricultural protectionism of the industrialised countries. Secondly, the information available throughout the primary industries about factors of all kinds affecting future demand and supply could be improved —long-term production plans, weather conditions, and developments in demand on the one side, and competing products and substitutes on the other. Thirdly, there could be further development of long-term commitments, whether in commodity futures dealings or in long-term contracts of a more general and non-discriminatory kind than those negotiated hitherto.

(i) *Access to markets in industrialised countries*

Better access to markets was one recommendation of the 1976 UNCTAD Conference[1] and of the Brandt Report.[2] The advantages both in promoting higher returns and larger sales for the poorer primary producers and in lessening the volatility of world markets hardly require argument. Although the support of agriculture is a highly political issue in most industrialised countries, opening their markets more freely and equally would be one of the most effective ways for them to help the poorer primary producers. They could, moreover, take this step at little (or even minus) cost to themselves if the consequential benefits to their own consumers and/or taxpayers were brought into the reckoning.

The improvement of market access for processed products is mentioned in the UNCTAD resolution. Apart from being desirable in itself, it might sometimes contribute a little to stabilisation by providing a significant local market for a locally-produced raw material. It is, however, unlikely to be a large factor in the demand for primary commodities as a whole.

(ii) *Provision of information*

Improving the flow of information is also mentioned in the UNCTAD resolution,[3] and in evidence submitted to the House of Lords Select Committee by, among others, the Institute of Development Studies at the University of Sussex.[4]

It would seem that the gathering and dissemination of information about production prospects is better organised for mineral than for agricultural products. The discovery of potentially large new oilfields, for example, is unlikely to remain

[1] Sub-para. 2(g) of Part III of the Conference resolution (UNCTAD IV, *Proceedings*, Vol. I, *loc. cit.*).

[2] *North-South, op. cit.*, pp. 99-100 and 'Summary of Recommendations', pp. 282-3.

[3] Sub-para. 2(c) of Part IV (UNCTAD IV, Vol. I, *loc. cit.*).

[4] *House of Lords Select Committee on Commodity Prices*, Vol. III: *Minutes of Evidence, op. cit.*, Appendix 5, pp. 615-19, especially pp. 616 and 618.

a secret for long—though the history of oil prices in the last few years suggests that the leading producers in the shape of the OPEC cartel may have under-estimated the potentialities of previously minor producers and/or their reactions to price rises. Organisations already exist in non-ferrous minerals for the provision both of current statistics and information about prospective developments. What follows therefore concentrates on agricultural products—including, of course, tree crops.

Information about short-term factors (such as worldwide crop prospects and immediate consumption trends) is obviously important for growers of annual crops, particularly where there is a sophisticated and complex system of agriculture and agricultural marketing which gives them a real choice about what to sow in the coming season. These conditions are typical of the industrialised rather than the developing countries. In the developing countries the pattern of production, even of annual crops, is apt to be more rigid—partly because of social habits and partly because of technical conditions. Switching from rice production to another crop is likely to be a major long-term decision, rather than a simple choice for one year, because of the lengthy repercussions, involving many individual producers, on irrigation systems, land layout (terracing, for example), and other adaptations.

For the tree crops and such products as sugar and sisal, as well as for mineral products, the length of the production cycle and the large initial capital investment required mean that, while the precise volume of production planned for a particular season may be varied according to information about short-term market prospects, decisions about switches to or from other lines of production have to be taken at much longer intervals. For that purpose the development plans of competitiors in world markets may be more important than current market conditions.

The author's own impression is that decisions on new capital development in primary production, whether by private organisations, governments or international agencies, are often taken with comparatively little consideration of developments planned or already in progress in other parts of the world. More dissemination of information about such developments could, therefore, help to check the tendency for new productive facilities to be installed as the result of a boom, only to come into operation in time to intensify the ensuing slump. Disseminating

[50]

such information seems a natural task for one or more of the interested international agencies—for agricultural products, perhaps a joint endeavour of the UN's Food and Agriculture Organisation (FAO) and the World Bank, which already undertake some similar activity. But futures markets also have a role to play here, since opportunities for successful speculators to make large profits provide a powerful incentive for the production of accurate information. Whichever organisations were to be responsible, however, it would be of decisive importance that information should be made available as promptly as possible if it was to be of help in influencing investment decisions.

(iii) *Long-term purchase arrangements*

The last approach to improving market operations is the development of long-term purchase arrangements. The term 'purchase arrangements' rather than 'contracts' is used so as to cover a wide spectrum of methods. It can cover, at one end, assurances of the reservation of markets made with varying degrees of formality to, at the other end, legally enforcible long-term contracts between private persons or corporations. It thus embraces not only long-term agreements *between* governments, such as the former Commonwealth Sugar Agreement and the EEC's Lomé Convention, but also the domestic arrangements which ensure reserved markets for agricultural producers in nearly all the highly-industrialised countries of the world.

These arrangements are not contractual in form, since they normally stem from legislation which could in theory be altered at any time—and which may, as in the UK before her entry into the Common Market, be based on annual reviews of prices, and possibly of quantities. Political considerations offer a high degree of assurance that they will be continued for long periods and modified only marginally in such reviews as take place. Arrangements of this kind, whether national or international in scope, have given a welcome measure of stability to the producers covered by them. That stability has encouraged the capital investment which has improved the efficiency of agricultural production in both the industrialised countries and the developing countries associated with the arrangements.

Such arrangements are, however, open to two substantial

criticisms. First, a considerable cost falls on consumers who are denied access to cheaper supplies. Secondly, producers in countries which do not enjoy the privileged positions created in the world's largest and wealthiest markets almost certainly receive lower prices and are certainly subjected to wider price fluctuations than if the total market open to them were larger. Essentially, the arrangements are a means of bestowing benefits on particular producers—primarily for political reasons—at the expense of the rest of the world. For free world markets, these arrangements are *de*-stabilising devices.

Promoting private contracts

What is more relevant to the stabilisation of world market prices, therefore, is the promotion of contractual arrangements for future sales between private individuals or corporations. For at least some primary products, future sales and purchases through terminal markets are common. They enable both producers and consumers to cover themselves against price variations over a period of a year or more ahead for at least some part of their output or their requirements.

The scale of futures market operations has increased substantially in recent years. Miss P. Ady, in evidence submitted to the House of Lords Committee,[1] quoted estimates compiled by W. Labys and H. C. Smith showing that trading in commodities of international origin (largely produced in the developing countries) on the US commodity exchanges rose from $5 billion to over $135 billion between 1960 and 1973; and trading on the London exchanges in the same period rose from £4 billion to £70 billion.[2] Much of this trading is speculative and the volume of trading recorded on the exchanges usually substantially exceeds the volume of physical sales made through them. Indeed, it usually exceeds the total volume of international trade in the commodities concerned. Miss Ady quoted data from the same source giving calculations of the ratio between total world imports and total trading on the New York and London exchanges; combined trans-

---

[1] 'A Note on Commodity Price Instability', Memorandum submitted by Miss P. Ady to the *House of Lords Select Committee on Commodity Prices,* Vol. III: *Minutes of Evidence, op. cit.,* p. 328, and Table I, p. 334.

[2] W. C. Labys and H. C. Smith, 'Speculation, Hedging and Commodity Price Behaviour', Institut Universitaire de Hautes Etudes Internationale Geneva, (mimeo), December 1974.

actions on the exchanges in the two cities amounted to nearly twice as much as the volume of imports of coffee, nearly four times as much for sugar, nearly 10 times for cocoa, and over 20 times for silver.

Between 1973 and 1982, the number of futures contracts traded on American commodity futures exchanges multiplied by a factor of six. Amongst internationally-traded commodities the growth of futures trading was not, however, quite so rapid. Even so, the New York Coffee and Cocoa Exchange, for example, doubled its contract volume, and trading in copper on the COMEX rose by more than four times in the same period.

Figures distinguishing 'speculative' from 'real' transactions are not available; indeed, they hardly could be since the difference between them is not easily defined. The data leave no doubt, however, that considerable use is being made of the futures markets by producers or by marketing boards selling on their behalf. Such extensive use implies that a considerable proportion of ouput is being sold well ahead of production and that producers are to that extent covering themselves against price fluctuations over a period of probably a year or so. Miss Ady also quoted from a study by C. Rockwell showing, from a survey of their experience over 18 years, that producers suffered a net loss on hedging transactions.[1] They may, however, have regarded that loss as a price worth paying for the element of certainty of cash return from transactions in futures.

The substantial use of futures on the commodity exchanges reinforces doubts whether actual returns to producers have varied as widely as the extremes of the price ranges quoted in this *Paper* suggest. It also raises the question whether more use of the exchanges by individual producers and producers' marketing organisations would make a major contribution to stabilising returns, if not recorded prices.

Speculative interest

There are, however, qualifications to the possible role of futures operations through commodity exchanges—as they are now

---

[1] C. Rockwell, 'Normal Backwardation, Forecasting and the Returns to Commodity Futures Trading', Proceedings of a Symposium on Price-Effects of Speculation in Organised Commodity Markets, Food Research Institute Studies, Supplement No. 4 (1967).

organised—in checking major price fluctuations. A considerable body of opinion suspects that the opportunities for speculation they provide to people with no direct interest in the use or production of the commodity concerned intensify rather than reduce price fluctuations. These 'outside speculators' are certainly more active in periods of wide price movements. Their more intense involvement, however, could equally be an effect rather than a cause of the exceptional fluctuations since they are naturally drawn in when the possibilities of profit are bigger. In their evidence to the House of Lords Committee, the representatives of various London commodity exchanges and trade federations, while not denying that outside speculation might occasionally exaggerate price movements, were in general firmly of the view that the participation of outside operators was valuable in enabling the exchanges to offer facilities for covering at least short-term risks to producers and users, and that the causes of the major price swings lay in the weather, government action or changes in demand.[1] Moreover, the outside speculator normally trades in futures, and not on the spot market, because he does not want to hold and finance large stocks. It is not clear how his operations affect spot prices, which are normally taken as the indicator of price instability.

It is by no means clear what effect forward selling by producers has on their actual receipts. Does the use of futures markets result in their losing less or more when prices are falling, or gaining more or less when prices are rising? More research into this question would be well worthwhile—research, for example, comparing futures prices for delivery at a date, say, 12 months ahead and spot prices actually prevailing when that date is reached. It might at least be possible to ascertain how well futures markets serve as guides to the direction of change. It would presumably follow that the effect on consumers would be the opposite of that on producers; that is, if the latter gained by selling forward, the former would lose. But if both sides experienced a lower degree of fluctuation, the improved stability might still make the forward transactions worthwhile for both.

---

[1] *House of Lords Select Committee on Commodity Prices*, Vol. I: *Report*, and Minutes of Evidence contained in Vols. II and III, *op. cit., passim.*

Longer-term guarantees

Even assuming that forward operations do normally enable producers to smooth out extreme price fluctuations, their use remains subject to a number of detailed limitations. Such operations are obviously not available to large numbers of small producers. They are suitable only for big production units or marketing organisations acting as intermediaries between the small producer and the buyer. Nor are they available for all primary products since their organisation depends upon the scope for dealing in a standardised commodity—or at least in one easily graded in relation to a defined standard, as with most metals. Because of grading problems there is, for instance, no terminal market in tea.

Finally—and more generally—the protection against unforeseen price changes which existing terminal markets offer does not extend over a long enough period to cover those price swings which are the major cause of concern. Futures quotations, as recorded in the press, are rarely for more than 18 months ahead. They are helpful in the planning of an annual production programme but not in deciding whether to plant a coffee or a cocoa tree, or build a sugar factory or open a new mine. Nor are they much help to government planners concerned about the possible variations in export earnings over a period of years.

Is it then out of the question that longer-term forward contracts—long enough to take realistic account of the lengthy production cycles characteristic of so many primary products—could be organised so as to offer more security to producers anywhere in the world?

Proposal for a broker-agency for long-term contracts

Implicit in this question is a suggestion for the creation of an international agency which would act as a broker in arranging contracts for longer periods than are available through the existing commodity exchanges. Producers of food and raw materials could put in offers of supply over such periods and in such quantities as they thought appropriate to their production prospects. Food-processors and manufacturers, on the other side, could ask for tenders. And the agency would do its best to bring the two sides together.

The attractiveness of dealing through such an agency would

be increased if it were able to offer guarantees of performance of the contracts it negotiated, analogous to those offered by commodity exchanges—or to the guarantees of payment the UK's Export Credits Guarantee Department (ECGD) offers on contracts for the supply of equipment by British manufacturers to overseas enterprises. There is no *prima facie* reason why more risk would be run in guaranteeing an Indonesian sugar factory's contract to supply sugar for some years ahead than in guaranteeing that same enterprise's contract to pay for a newly-equipped factory—as the ECGD is doing today.

The world economy is nothing like stable enough to foresee that long-term contracts of the kind envisaged might cover the whole, or even the major part, of international transactions in primary produce. But they could prove particularly useful in commodities subject to the long-term production cycles which, it has been suggested, are partly responsible for wide price fluctuations. They would basically constitute an extension of ordinary marketing processes to meet the special circumstances of such commodities, without interfering with the fundamental allocatory functions of the market.

Long-term contract agency

The concept of such a 'Long-Term Contract Agency' is novel, and it may be argued that, were there a widespread desire on the part of producers and consumers to enter into long-term contracts, ordinary commercial agents would already be negotiating them. The element of guarantee, however, would be something commercial agents might be reluctant to provide. The offer of such a facility would at least test the value placed by both producers and consumers on stability, in contrast to accepting widely varying prices with more or less equal chances of a large profit or a severe loss. Sometimes at least, it would perhaps be discovered that immediate consumers (processors or manufacturers) placed a lower value on stability than producers, and that they were only interested in contracts at a price lower than the probable mid-point of expectations. Producers might still think it worthwhile doing a deal on such a basis if it protected them from the danger of a catastrophic loss resulting from price falls. Equally, manufacturers who were more concerned with the continuity of supply of an essential raw material than with the small percentage of their total costs it represented, might be willing to pay something extra to protect themselves against an interruption of their production flow in a period of acute shortage of the material.

Such a scheme would require to be worked out in much more detail, particularly since the detailed provisions would necessarily vary for different commodities. The term of any contract would also need close examination. Although five years sounds attractive in many ways, it might be thought too long for guarantees to be offered; shorter periods might be preferred, at any rate at the outset of a scheme. One special provision would certainly be required in the light of recent economic history, namely, some adjustment of contract prices to allow for price rises attributable to general inflation between the date of contract and the date of performance.

Summary of proposals

The commodity price problem is many-sided and it is most unlikely that any one line of action will solve it. The following steps would, however, contribute to its solution:

(a) A widening of the markets open to countries most dependent on primary production (by reducing those parts of the total market reserved for protected producers);

(b) Stock-management schemes, provided they are operated with sufficient caution and backed up by export controls;

(c) A systematic promotion of long-term contracts which, while they cannot guarantee income from exports in the longer run, can mitigate the short-term impact of fluctuations and afford more time for necessary adjustments to production;

(d) The making available of as much information as possible about production and consumption trends to assist the new production plans of individual enterprises.

SEVEN: Summary and Conclusions

1. Discussion of schemes to regulate international trade in primary commodities has a long history. Schemes came into operation for a small number of commodities during the period 1919 to 1939. The World Monetary and Economic Conference of 1933 gave a general blessing to such schemes and approved a fairly simple set of principles by which they should be conducted. Since 1945 further schemes have been discussed—and some brought into operation—for a larger number of commodities. The discussion of a more general and comprehensive approach to the establishment of a 'new order' of international trade in commodities has been the main preoccupation of the United Nations Conference on Trade and Development. In 1976 UNCTAD IV agreed to recommend a wide range of proposals in this field.

2. The principles and proposals adopted in 1933 and 1976, like most of the public discussion, are characterised by a basically 'distributive' approach. They are concerned with prices and international markets as mechanisms for securing a pattern of distribution of incomes, not as mechanisms for securing a balance between supply and demand and an allocation of resources to different kinds of production reasonably in line with consumer preferences. This *Hobart Paper* has analysed the difficulties of devising a satisfactory alternative mechanism to the market for the latter purpose, and the consequential problems encountered by regulation schemes.

3. The well-established susceptibility of primary commodity markets to wide fluctuations in prices is to a large extent due to certain features of the demand for them, and to the technical conditions of their production which make both supply and demand relatively inelastic in response to changes in price—and, in particular, often *slow* to react to such changes—so that shortages and, still more, surpluses require a substantial time to be corrected. The disadvantages of the degree of fluctuation are real (although there is little

[58]

evidence for the common allegation that it results in reduced investment), and it would be in the mutual interest of producers and consumers to lessen it.

4. Proposals to limit price fluctuations are frequently linked explicitly (as in the resolution of the 1933 Conference) or implicitly to the object of raising average prices for primary producers as part of a more general design to redistribute wealth between the richer and the poorer countries.[1] It is an imperfect and haphazard route to that end because, although the poorer (or developing) countries are commonly largely dependent on primary products, there is also a lot of such production in the richer, industrialised countries. Moreover, the poorest communities of all, such as many in India, usually have little contact with world markets and little to gain from an increase in world market prices. A general rise in commodity prices above market-clearing levels would, therefore, be *inefficient* as a way of transferring wealth from the richer to the poorer, and additional controls would be required to cope with the inevitable increase of production and creation of surpluses.

5. In considering possible lines of action, this *Paper* has focussed attention on those concerned with the general international market for a particular commodity, leaving aside partial schemes such as national marketing boards which may operate to smooth out prices for producers in a single country. It has also discussed special long-term arrangements between individual importing and exporting countries which may alleviate the problems of a particular group of producers only by exacerbating the price fluctuations encountered by exporters to that residual part of the world market which remains open. Finally, the *Paper* has examined compensation schemes which aim to offset the consequences of price fluctuations for the export receipts of selected countries.

6. The very real practical drawbacks of quota regulation and stockpiling schemes have been reviewed—especially the problems of: choosing the price target or targets to govern the increase or reduction of quotas and the purchase or release of stocks; fixing and adjusting quotas, particularly when a large number of existing or potential exporting

---

[1] The Brandt Report, *North-South, op. cit.*, is a more recent example.

countries are involved; and, for stockpiling schemes, the practical problems of storage.

7. Apart from these important administrative difficulties, there are basic objections in principle to both quota regulation and stockpiling schemes. Stockpiling could be successful in holding prices within a moderate range provided market pressures were not such as to push the equilibrium, or market-clearing, price far beyond the top or bottom of the agreed range. To prevent prices rising to exceptional heights in times of acute real or apprehended shortage would entail holding very large stocks, while arresting severe falls in periods of substantial excess production would require either unlimited financial resources or quota control. Yet it is the wide fluctuations, not the moderate ones, which people want to control. Schemes of quota control, either independently of stockpiling or in support of it (supposing the practical difficulties of agreement on quotas and their enforcement were overcome), would almost certainly freeze the pattern of output and prevent new developments. They broadly serve the interests of the 'haves' against the 'have-nots' in the world of primary production.

8. As a means of helping the less developed parts of the world, commodity regulation and stockpiling schemes are likely to be, at best, cumbrous and inefficient and, at worst, positively harmful to the poorest communities, whilst imposing costs on consumers everywhere. To quote the submission to the House of Lords Committee by Professors Bauer and Myint:

> 'Nor is commodity policy a suitable instrument for wealth transfers from rich countries to poor countries. If such transfers are thought desirable, the appropriate method is that of cash grants which can be integrated into the budgetary processes of the donor countries.'[1]

9. More cost-effective ways of mitigating wide price fluctuations would be to expand commodity markets and improve the services they offer—rather than seeking to distort their operation or replace them. For example:

    (i) Markets could be widened by abandoning the reser-

---

[1] P. T. Bauer and H. Myint, 'Commodity Prices', *House of Lords Select Committee on Commodity Prices*, Vol. III: *Minutes of Evidence, 7 July—15 December 1976*, HL 165-iii, HMSO, 1977, Appendix 4, p. 614.

vation of national markets to national producers, especially in the industrialised countries, thereby giving more opportunities to producers in the developing countries, creating larger markets to take the strain of unexpected changes in demand or supply, and reducing the cost of tariff protection, subsidies, and so on to consumers and/or taxpayers.

(ii) Information could be more systematically collated and disseminated—perhaps by international agencies such as the FAO and the World Bank—about actual and prospective developments likely to affect demand or supply, including plans for significant additions to total output.

(iii) Some of the problems of commodities with long production cycles (tree-crops, mines, etc.) could be met by setting up an international agency charged with seeking to negotiate long-term supply contracts available to all producers and consumers; thus all producers would be offered the prospect of that degree of protection against price fluctuations hitherto available only to selected and favoured producers through the Commonwealth Sugar Agreement, the Lomé Convention and similar arrangements.

TOPICS FOR DISCUSSION

1. What are the special characteristics of primary products which determine their market behaviour?

2. What possible objectives might be achieved by trying to reduce the volatility of commodity prices?

3. What types of regulatory devices have so far been tried out to do this?

4. How are regulatory devices supposed to achieve their objectives?

5. Contrast the principles laid down at the 1933 World Economic Conference with those agreed at the UNCTAD Conference in 1976.

6. In what ways do the industrialised countries hinder the exports from primary producing countries?

7. Is there scope for improving the flow of information in commodity markets?

8. Describe how long-term contracts might be developed by an international agency. What would they be intended to achieve?

9. Does speculation intensify or reduce price fluctuations?

FURTHER READING

Bauer, P. T., and Yamey, B. S., *The Economics of Underdeveloped Countries,* Cambridge Economic Handbooks, Cambridge University Press, London, 1957.

——, 'Organised Commodity Stabilisation with Voluntary Participation', *Oxford Economic Papers,* March 1964, reprinted in Bauer and Yamey, *Markets, Market Control and Marketing Reform,* Weidenfeld and Nicolson, London, 1968.

Brandt Commission, The, *North-South: A Programme for Survival,* The Report of the Independent Commission on International Development Issues under the Chairmanship of Willy Brandt, Pan Books, London, 1980.

——, *Common Crisis—North-South: Co-operation for World Recovery,* The Brandt Commission 1983, Pan Books, London, 1983.

Caine, Sir Sydney, *Prices for Primary Producers,* Hobart Paper 24, Institute of Economic Affairs, London, 1963 (Second Edition, 1966).

Goss, B. A., and Yamey, B. S., *The Economics of Futures Trading,* Macmillan, London, 1976.

Grondona, L. St. Clare, *Utilizing World Abundance,* George Allen and Unwin, London, 1958.

House of Lords Select Committee on Commodity Prices:
    Vol. I: *Report of the Committee,* HL 165-i, HMSO, 1977;
    Vol. II: *Minutes of Proceedings,* Session 1975-76, and *Minutes of Evidence,* 18 February-30 June 1976, HL 165-ii, HMSO, 1977;
    Vol. III: *Minutes of Evidence,* 7 July-15 December 1976, and *Appendices to the Minutes of Evidence,* HL 165-iii, HMSO, 1977.

MacBean, Alasdair I., *Export Instability and Economic Development*, George Allen and Unwin, London, 1966.

UNCTAD, *Proceedings of the United Nations Conference on Trade and Development*, Fourth Session, Nairobi, 5-31 May 1976, United Nations, New York, 1977.

Yamey, B. S., 'Commodity Futures Markets, Hedging and Speculation', in *City Lights: Essays on financial institutions and markets in the City of London*, IEA Readings No. 19, Institute of Economic Affairs, London, 1979.